IMAGES
of America

HESS'S DEPARTMENT
STORE

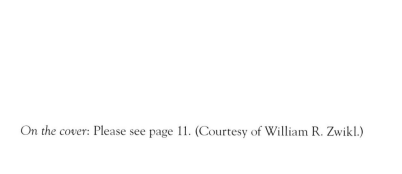

On the cover: Please see page 11. (Courtesy of William R. Zwikl.)

IMAGES
of America

HESS'S DEPARTMENT STORE

Frank A. Whelan and Kurt D. Zwikl

ARCADIA
PUBLISHING

Copyright © 2008 by Frank A. Whelan and Kurt D. Zwikl
ISBN 978-0-7385-6275-9

Published by Arcadia Publishing
Charleston, South Carolina

Printed in the United States of America

Library of Congress Catalog Card Number: 2008928785

For all general information contact Arcadia Publishing at:
Telephone 843-853-2070
Fax 843-853-0044
E-mail sales@arcadiapublishing.com
For customer service and orders:
Toll-Free 1-888-313-2665

Visit us on the Internet at www.arcadiapublishing.com

INTRODUCTION

For anyone who knew Allentown and the Lehigh Valley in the 20th century, Hess's was more than just a place to go shopping. Starting on February 19, 1897, when it opened to the snappy sound of the Allentown Band playing John Philip Sousa marches, to its last moments in 2000 under the ball of a wrecking crane, Hess's was always a spectacle.

According to the story that the local newspapers reprinted every year on the store's anniversary, Hess Brothers began when Max Hess Sr., a German-Jewish immigrant from Perth Amboy, New Jersey, walked down Allentown's Hamilton Street in 1896.

When he got to Ninth and Hamilton Streets, two blocks beyond the growing city's retail district, he noticed virgin territory with only a hotel and several lumberyards. This, he went back home and told his partner and brother Charles, was the land of business opportunity.

At first glance, Allentown seemed an unlikely place for a store like Hess's to thrive. Founded in 1762, the town was largely populated by conservative Pennsylvania Germans who might be called the original "if it ain't broke don't fix it" people. They were known, perhaps unfairly, for not wanting to accept new ideas or habits.

Max Hess Sr. might already have been well aware of what he was dealing with. He grew up in Germany. Among the things that he seemed to know and apparently passed on to his son was that if one gave the Pennsylvania German people quality, they would be among the most loyal shoppers a department store owner could have.

The Hesses set themselves up in what was basically a small dry goods space inside the Grand Central Hotel. Opening day for Hess Brothers, as it was then called, was February 19, 1897. It is safe to say there was probably not a store opening in Allentown that was anything like it. On that morning, shoppers were greeted by the Allentown Band playing the latest songs by Sousa, the country's leading composer of popular music.

With the "Washington Post March" playing in the background, they were greeted by Hess Brothers' neatly lined shelves of goods. Chances were good that at that time the first Hess's did not look much different then many other dry goods stores of the day.

How does one explain the early success of Hess Brothers? Perhaps the most significant thing was advertising. Max Hess Sr. did a lot of it right from the start. The newspapers quite naturally were pleased to have such a large advertiser, and to judge from the space they filled in the papers around 1900, the store must have been among their biggest.

Max Hess Sr. also had a genuine desire in that Progressive Era environment to do good for his adopted community. Whether it was starting the drive that led to the founding of the Jewish

Community Center, the Allentown Public Library, or the first Reformed Jewish Temple, he was there.

Another factor that made Hess Brothers stand out among local merchants was what might be called class. Allentown and Lehigh Valley dry goods store operators were from a largely rural background. The tradition was not to appear to be showy or pushy. There was a naturally skeptical approach to the "big city."

But by the dawn of the 20th century, Allentown was beginning to see itself as a city. From Mack trucks to Bethlehem Steel, the region was industrializing. People had more money in their pockets than ever, and the consumer goods revolution of the 1920s, complete with installment buying, was making inroads even into the Lehigh Valley.

Hess Brothers understood and catered to these newly emerging longings. Perhaps the best example was Hess's French Room. Charles Hess was probably its creator. He had an interest in fashion, particularly French fashion.

Judging from the local newspapers of the early 20th century, one of the high points of the fashion seasons was Charles Hess's trips to Paris. In detailed gossipy articles, he discussed what the fashionable woman of the French capital were wearing in the Bois de Boulogne or at the opening of the Paris Opera. It was a foundation on which Max Hess Jr. would build.

The real core of Hess's success seems to have been in their sales. They were masters at offering the public quality goods for less. The store's bargain sales were legendary from the start.

The store expanded. Rather than construct new buildings, the Hesses decided to slowly annex those near them one by one.

By 1915, Hess's store came to dominate the northeast corner of Ninth and Hamilton Streets. Although the building-by-building process was economical at the time, it did lead to some problems in the future. In order to walk around the store, shoppers had to walk up a step from one floor to another. And until the late 1930s, when Max Hess Jr. encased the property in a sleek art moderne–style facade, it presented an odd face to the streetscape.

Although Max Hess Sr. died in 1922, and his brother Charles died in 1929, their legacy passed to the generation of managers they trained. They continued the pioneering ways of the store's founders.

Like many retailers across the country, Hess's executives were caught off guard by the Great Depression of the 1930s. It was in 1932 that Max Hess Jr. left Muhlenberg College to step into his family's legacy. In many ways, a more skilled merchandiser than either his father or his uncle, he made the store his trademark and identity factor.

In time, Max Hess Jr. assumed the role of merchant prince. He and the store became one. In a way, he projected his fantasy about the store to a larger public. Hess was a master showman like a Broadway producer. A lover of the limelight and as starstruck by Hollywood as most Americans, he had an instinctive understanding of what the shoppers of his era wanted: bargains, razzle-dazzle, and "just a little touch of star quality."

By the late 1940s, the store had escalators worthy of a New York department store. The big splash was the sign, a 45-foot-tall, eight-ton giant with letters seven feet high whose 2,250 lightbulbs flashed out the name Hess. Said to be the largest sign of its kind between New York and Chicago, it gave a special big-city air to Allentown.

The interior of the store was Hess's stage set. Giant crystal chandeliers hung from the ceiling. Artworks, all of them for sale, decorated corners of the store. Starlets and stars of the stage, screen, and television appeared as Hess's guests, hawking his merchandise. Even television's Superman George Reeves and the exotic actress Zsa Zsa Gabor were draws for Hess's merchandising style.

When the topless women's bathing suit craze broke into the news in 1964, Hess's quickly ordered them. Nobody in Allentown bought them, but everybody knew Hess's had them first.

There were many other less controversial ways the Hess family promoted the store. Flower shows worthy of an exotic tropical jungle and beautiful animated Christmas displays with puppets imported from Italy where there to entertain and delight shoppers.

From 1951 to 1996, Hess's also operated its Patio Restaurant, known for its large portions and rich, sweet strawberry pie. It kept shoppers in the store instead of having them wander outside looking for a place to eat. It also added to Hess's aura and its slogan, "Hess's has the best of everything."

In 1968, for reasons that are still largely unknown but widely rumored, Max Hess Jr. did the unthinkable—he sold the store to Philip I. Berman, a multitalented businessman and art collector. A year later, Max Hess Jr. died. He was 58 years old.

Berman was not a retailer by background. What he and Max Hess Jr. had in common, albeit in different ways, was a flare for publicity. Unlike Max Hess, however, it was artists and politicians rather than television and movie stars that were Berman's interests. With his wife, Muriel, he had a magnificent collection of modern and contemporary art.

Berman's politics as a liberal Democrat made him just a slightly more controversial figure than Max Hess Jr. Berman owned the store into the 1980s, bringing to it artists and prominent political figures of the day, including former vice president Hubert Humphrey and former president Jimmy Carter.

In the 1980s, Hess's became a part of the Crown American chain. Soon Hess stores were all over the eastern United States, but with the growth of big box stores, Hess's days were numbered.

It was 1996 when the store was closed by its new owners, Bon-Ton of York, and was torn down to make way for a new office and restaurant space building designed by Robert A. M. Stern for the PPL electric company.

For the generations who still remember the memory of Hess's, what one called "Hollywood on Hamilton Street" will be forever green. This book is a way of saying thanks to Max Hess Sr. and Max Hess Jr., and all those who made it possible.

Hess's fashion shows fascinated their customer base and the greater Lehigh Valley community. Creative work in the darkroom allowed Hess's photographer, William R. (Bill) Zwikl, to print this pastel-like image he took of a model at a Hess's import fashion show at the Americana Hotel in New York City in the 1960s. Former Hess's president Irwin Greenberg said of Zwikl after his death in 1986, "He recorded some of the most significant moments in Hess's history on film. His contributions to Hess's growth and fashion presentation were immeasurable. He accompanied me on numerous buying trips including Europe and his photography of the most elite in high fashion and exclusive events truly set him apart from others in the field."

One

HESS'S EARLY YEARS

From the 1900s to the 1970s, there was no busier spot in downtown Allentown than the northeast corner of Ninth and Hamilton Streets occupied by Hess's department store. Here at the city's commercial center, shown in the early 1960s, the third-largest city in Pennsylvania's heart throbbed like a miniature midtown Manhattan.

By 1907, Hess Brothers staff had gone from being largely male to largely female. These ladies at the notions counter are Gertie Miller (left) and Mary Wertz. Throughout its nearly 100-year history, Hess's was known for concern for its staff's welfare.

The menswear department at Hess Brothers in 1907 was presided over by the dapper clerks Herb Davis (left) and H. F. Newhard. A Hess's bargain sale offering 50¢ shirts for 35¢ was underway.

In 1907, Hess's was already 10 years old and had made a name for itself as offering everything. These young men stand ready to offer help in the burnt wood department.

These nurses' and governess' uniforms were both stylish and professional for 1907, and Hess's had them.

The interior of Hess's baby carriage department was not much in 1907, but the fringed carriages would be priceless today.

Even in 1907, Hess's was known for enhancing the shopping experience. Sweeping spaces and potted palms in place of dark, dusty shelves were part of it.

These proper women sales clerks were ready to offer whatever the stylish early-20th-century women could want in undergarments.

Hess's was famous for its bargain sales as far back as 1907. These high-button shoes were all the rage.

Is this a first-class parlor suite on the *Titanic*? No, it is Hess's French Room around 1912, a perfect place for a Gibson girl to pick out the latest fashion.

Butterrick patterns were popular for woman who wanted to make their own dresses. An attentive Hess's sales clerk is ready to help.

Period furniture was very popular in the early 20th century. Here are some of the replicas of 18th-century chairs used by customers at Hess's shoe department in 1926.

Hess's French Room, shown in this 1927 photograph, resembled one of the era's grand hotels. Electric light assured dirt could not be hidden.

Hess was among the first stores in the Lehigh Valley to deliver by truck. Here are some of the trucks in the parking garage in 1925.

The early 1920s had arrived, but Hess's was aware that not every woman was ready to give up her corset. A pile of them at a table on the right were on sale for $2 to $1.50.

Cloche hats were the trademark of the sophisticated woman of the 1920s. Hess's offered many choices for a daring flapper.

By 1927, Hess's was booming and needed to expand its warehouse. This photograph shows the excavation for it underway behind the store.

The 1930s was a high-style decade, and Hess's was there with this art deco milk bar. That must be Daisy over the bar.

If someone lost a heel on a shoe while walking down Hamilton Street in 1933, Hess's was ready with shoe repairs "while-U-wait" at this stylish stand.

Need a close shave and do not have time for the barber? In the spring of 1936, Hess was offering the latest thing, an electric razor. Note the tie and checked shirt of the stylish young clerk.

Donuts were popular in the 1930s, and this young woman could offer one of Hess Brothers own make. Plain were 25¢, decorated cost 35¢.

On a winter day around 1930, what better way was there to spend the time than shopping for food at Hess's grocery?

Water carafes, electric grillettes (small electric grills), and chaffing dishes were all set for Hess's customers in the 1930s.

Bargains at Hess's were always popular and never more so than at Christmastime. In this photograph, the store is decorated in the 1930s for the holidays, with gift suggestions from stylish lamps with fringed shades to colorful purses.

Two

HESS'S INSIDE AND OUT

Hess's began as a series of smaller buildings that were merged into one, and it gradually took over almost the entire north side of Hamilton Street from the middle of the 800 block to Ninth Street. This photograph shows it as it looked before a rummage sale in 1908.

A group of shoppers waiting outside Hess's front door before a sale was an old tradition. Here is a group waiting to get in around 1909.

By the early 1920s, unity had been brought to Hess's facade by painting all of its buildings white. The floors of these buildings did not always match, so Hess's shoppers often had to walk up and down a step at times, although few seemed to mind.

The Hess facade urges shoppers to buy bonds during World War II. This photograph offers a fine view of the store's art moderne facade added by Max Hess Jr. in 1939 to further unite the building.

After World War II, Hess's was a popular Christmas stop, complete with trees over the doors.

Angles dance across the art moderne facade of Hess's in the 1980s at Christmastime.

Downtown Hess's store exterior is pictured in the 1970s, just before the creation of the Hamilton Mall. The sign has been taken down to make way for mall canopies.

Hamilton Mall construction gets under way in 1973. The Hamilton Mall, which was a modernesque arcade of overhead canopies from Tenth Street to Sixth Street, was a feature of Allentown's cityscape from 1974 to 2000.

Pictured here is a Christmas display for Hess's window around 1964.

Christmas was always a Hess's specialty. Characters out of Charles Dickens's *A Christmas Carol* greeted shoppers in the 1960s.

Displays at Hess's were not just limited to the inside of the store. Here 1960s Christmas-season shoppers are greeted by a holiday-themed fantasy over the front door.

Hess's giant sign, a community icon from 1947 to 1973, dominates Hamilton Street at Christmastime.

Pictured here is Hess's Christmas exterior design for Christmas 1954.

This Hess's sign was designed to lure in bargain shoppers around 1962.

This view of Hamilton Street was taken from Hess's during construction of the Hilton Hotel in 1980.

Here is a view up Allentown's Ninth Street taken from Hess's back window. Frank's restaurant, where the sign is at right, was a popular local eatery. According to one story, for years its owner successfully resisted efforts by Max Hess Jr. to purchase it in order to expand the store.

This building in the 800 block of Linden Street was the nerve center of Hess's advertising and publicity operations. Photographer Bill Zwikl had his studio here. Behind the building was Hess's warehouse, a huge structure built in the 1920s.

Hamilton Street around 1964 is pictured here. The huge Hess's sign that dominates the streetscape and the Cadillac with tail fins evoke the era in Allentown like few other icons can.

The Boyd movie theater was part of a chain of theaters in the Lehigh Valley. This one was located on Ninth Street in Allentown across from Hess's. The theater was featuring a Fox Movietone newsreel of Max Hess Jr. giving a film of the inauguration of Pennsylvania governor William Scranton to the new governor in 1963.

For Max Hess Jr. and Philip I. Berman, the interior of the store was as important as the windows. An Asian motif complete with urns from the mystic exotic East dominate the women's department.

Christmas was always an important time for Hess's. Here some manikins spread the Christmas spirit to shoppers in the men's department.

Angels who have heard on high spread the peace and joy of the holiday season with Hess's shoppers. The store's elaborate displays were part of the Hess's experience.

Under the crystal chandeliers hung with garland for Christmas in the early 1960s, shoppers take advantage of those last-minute holiday sales.

On Christmas Eve in the 1960s, Hess's employees sing Christmas carols before the opening of the store.

Dolls were also a Hess special. Here in 1966, Anita Dreisbach, holding Debra Ann with Cheryl Lynn kneeling, wife and children of Hess's merchandise manager John Dreisbach, are shown at the doll counter with a Hess's employee.

John Dreisbach (left) presents Bill Marine, Hess's toy buyer, with Hess's service pin on the fourth floor. The toy department was a regional attraction for the families and children of the Lehigh Valley.

The giant toy soldiers that became a Hess's trademark for Christmas began at Hess's South Mall store on the south side of Allentown in 1974.

A ceremony at the opening of one of Hess's many suburban mall stores in the 1980s is shown here.

The day in 1972 when former president Harry S. Truman died, Hess's featured this tribute in its display window. The photograph was taken by Hess's photographer, Bill Zwikl, when Truman campaigned in Allentown during the famous whistle-stop presidential visit of 1948.

The energy crises of the 1970s caused Hess's to close their display windows on the Ninth Street side of the store. In this image, the late-afternoon sun casts a shadow of one of Allentown's well-known streetlamps on the blocked-up display windows.

Three

THE DISPLAY WINDOWS

World War II's Rosie the Riveter made wearing pants permissible for many women. Hess's got into the swing of things in 1944 with this paint display window.

From the 1950s to the 1980s, Hess's vice president Wolfgang Otto was the master of design at Hess's display windows. One of his many 1970s creations was a series of tributes to American fashion designers. This one honors Bill Blass.

Otto's sense of style and lighting echoed the image of glamour and sophistication that was the store's trademark. Here is one window honoring the designer Sant'Angelo.

Oscar de la Renta was an icon of mid-20th-century fashion. Wolfgang Otto's display windows, which were simple but elegant, never outshined the fashions that were on display.

Hess's fashions, such as this outfit by Stephen Burrows, were not something that many people would want to wear, but they were something that shoppers were glad were in the store.

Wolfgang Otto's work was not always high fashion. Here is a display of casual dresses that was more in local taste when it was done in 1958.

In a series of windows from the 1970s, titled, That's My Sport, Otto uses other items related to sports to accent women's fashion for Hess's.

Billie Jean King and women's tennis were all the rage when Otto designed this window for the That's My Sport series.

The sail display window in the That's My Sport series features a poster with a face that slightly resembles Diane Keaton, an actress very much in the news at that time. And the sporty outfits suggest a modern woman-on-the-go theme.

Foreign travel was still glamorous in the 1960s, and Wolfgang Otto has dotted the globe with international landmarks from the fashion capitals of Europe for the women's shoe display window.

Adventure was the theme for this display window, with bold prints from exotic Thailand in the 1970s.

Cutting-edge fashion was a Hess's trademark from the beginning. Here is a window display of an exotic dress by designer Bergin Usberk in the 1970s.

Dresses that one might see at the opening of the opera at Lincoln Center or a White House dinner could also be found in Hess's display windows.

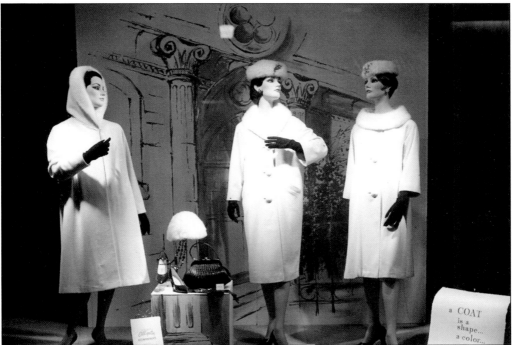

Wolfgang Otto has chosen an exotic look that is almost reminiscent of *Doctor Zhivago* to highlight these women's winter coats at Hess's window display in the 1960s.

With the ocean liner *France* looming in the background, this Hess's display window suggests its new Voila dresses for girls are right off the boat from Paris.

An imaginative rendering of the Café Flore, an actual Paris sidewalk café, is the setting Wolfgang Otto has chosen for the Hess's display window for these dresses by Mamselle.

These elegant chiffon summer dresses seem to float in the breeze in this window display by Otto in the 1960s.

Summer white for a garden party was still the fashion in the 1950s when Otto did this window display.

A world's fair was taking place in Brussels in 1958, and Hess's had just the right black-and-white fashions for female fairgoers, including the correct hat.

Easter was almost as big a fashion holiday as Christmas for Hess's. Here the Easter bunny of the late 1950s joins a group of fashionable little girls for the Easter parade.

Little girls still wore nightshirts to bed in the late 1950s, and here are some that were on sale for baby-boomer kids in Hess's display windows.

Her dress is pink, and Wolfgang Otto has chosen to make the early-1960s display window fit for an angel.

The Christmas past meets Christmas present in this chic window display of the early 1960s. A Victorian maiden and her modern sister share a Hess's display window.

Four

HESS'S FASHION

Max Hess Jr. learned early the power of television. Here are a number of Hess's fashion models getting ready to appear on Philadelphia television during the 1952 Christmas season with the store's public relations man Max "Maggie" Levine. The reason for the trampoline is unknown.

Philadelphia's Logan Square was the focal point of this 1976 bicentennial fashion show by Hess's. Benjamin Franklin (right) is even on hand to enjoy the show hosted by television celebrity Mike Douglas, seated at left.

Hess's models for the bicentennial fashion show pose for photographers as they get ready to walk down the runway to a waiting crowd.

With a set showing Paris's Notre Dame cathedral in the background, Hess's fashion guru Gerry Golden instructs a model before a televised Hess's fashion special in the mid-1960s.

With India's exotic Taj Mahal as a backdrop, a Hess's model gets final directions for an appearance on a late-1960s television show.

It was the spring of 1968 when these two Hess's models were about to model two of the high-fashion creations of the store's French Room.

Santa Claus is part of this 1970s *Hess's Christmas Circus*, a seasonal television show on fashion put on by Hess's. The children are probably wondering when they get to tour the store's famous toy department. The show was broadcast from Philadelphia's Channel 6 and hosted by Jim O'Brien. To the left of Santa Claus is Hess's fashion specialist Yvonne Burbage.

Swimwear may not have been at the top of everybody's Christmas list, but Hess's wanted to remind shoppers that it had plenty in its store.

Bill Weber, master of ceremonies for Hess's Christmas fashion show, talks into the boom microphone at the start of a holiday fashion show.

Bikini bathing suits and Christmas trees may seem like a strange combination but not at *Hess's Christmas Circus*.

The display of fashion at Hess's was always tasteful and elegant. Here is the French Room around 1960.

Although high fashion was important to Hess's, the store never forgot that their customer base was more conservative. Here a group of women admire a Hess's model in something they might wear during Pres. Dwight D. Eisenhower's era.

Longwood Gardens was the setting for this fashion show around 1950. The longer, New Look dresses were popular in those years.

Never wanting to miss a chance, in 1968, Hess's sent out three models on Hamilton Street with the names of that year's presidential candidates, Richard Nixon, Hubert Humphrey, and Eugene McCarthy, on their matching dresses.

On the steps of the lobby of Allentown's Americus Hotel, this Hess's model displays an outfit in keeping with the space's Spanish-Moorish decor.

Hess's photographer, Bill Zwikl, was often called on to try new techniques to create exciting and interesting pictures for newspaper advertisements. Here is one unique photograph from the 1960s that gives the model an unearthly quality.

Another interesting exposure shows a Hess's model apparently moving to the beat of music while dancing. It tends to also show how the dress, despite its length, can move in conjunction with the model's body.

A surreal park is the setting of this unusual exposure by Bill Zwikl. The three models, one in bell bottoms, another in high boots, and a third in a shift dress, show the elegance of the designs while at the same time giving them an otherworldly air.

Rome and Paris were centers of fashion in the 1960s, with fancy, long dresses and flowing wraps being all the rage. This Hess's model, placed perhaps in the store, suggests Jackie Kennedy–style elegance and Sophia Loren–style glamour.

Max Hess Jr. believed in bringing fashion to the customer. Here is Hess's Fashion Caravan bus in the 1950s. The bus brought fashion shows to communities around the Lehigh Valley as well as Philadelphia and New York City.

Hess's fashion models were icons in the Lehigh Valley. Here one models the latest look for a local woman's group in the 1950s.

Hess's master of fashion Gerry Golden conducts a show of Hess's models in the 1960s.

Longwood Gardens, a former estate of the DuPont family in southeastern Pennsylvania and now a public garden, was the setting for this Hess's model to show high fashion in the 1950s.

This lovely model shows off the latest item from Paris around 1964. Even if bargain sales drew bigger crowds, the high fashion was high profile, and Hess's made the most of it.

This Hess's model shows the latest high-fashion casual wear of the 1960s.

Ball gowns were all the rage. Here fashion director Gerry Golden gets a model ready for a photo shoot. While Hess's had shows at both indoor and outdoor locations at different times of the year, shoppers could catch a glimpse of the latest fashions while having lunch at the Patio Restaurant six days a week.

High fashion, beautiful and sophisticated models, and stylized backgrounds were all trademarks of Hess's in its heyday.

The Lehigh Valley Railroad's *Black Diamond*, the signature train of the line that carried many Allentown residents back and forth to New York, was the setting for this 1950s Hess's fashion show, featuring a mink beach robe, swim suits, and dinner gowns.

Golden helps a model get accessories ready for a 1960s fashion show. Golden was known throughout the European fashion capitals as someone with a keen sense of style and taste who brought those looks to Hess's of Allentown. At the same time, European designers came to know Hess's as well. The store advertised that it had offices in "London, Paris, Rome" and constantly sent Golden and many store buyers to these locations to purchase the latest fashions.

A Hess's model is trimmed in fur in a winter fashion photo shoot in 1972.

Hess's model Pat Kauffman displays her dress before a newspaper photograph event around 1960 in this holiday promotion advertisement.

hess's
P. O.
Reminder!
DEC. 10th
DEADLINE!
FOR
AIR-MAILING
GIFTS
to G.I.'s
OVERSEAS

A Hess's fashion model reminds shoppers to send packages to 1950s GI's overseas early. While Hess's fashion shows were often extravagant events, many models were photographed for newspaper advertisements promoting fashions that were available for sale in the store.

Max Hess Jr.'s attempt to track down the latest in fashions for his store went worldwide. Here from left to right are Hess's employees Boris Weisman, Joyce Mourat, Irwin Greenberg, Doris Hockman, and Bill Zwikl as they get ready to attend the Scandinavian Fashion Week about to be held in Copenhagen, Denmark.

Hess's fashion and toy show was broadcast from Philadelphia's Channel 6 in the 1970s. The children are sons and daughters of Hess's employees.

Five

HESS'S ADVERTISING AND PROMOTIONS

Hess's flower shows were major events in the 1960s and 1970s and often featured a special guest. This photograph, taken at the 1970 show, pictures Angie Brooks, president of the United Nations General Assembly, that year's honored guest.

Santa Claus's arrival at Hess's was always special. Here the jolly old elf "lands" in an early-1960s flying saucer at the Allentown Fairgrounds racetrack.

Santa Claus is greeted by spacemen seeking toys in the early 1960s.

Max Hess Jr. is surrounded by children of employees at Hess's toy council in New York. Hess bought toys to be sold at the store based on what the children liked. Featured in the photograph with Hess are Larry Clymer on the left, Wayne Holben holding the sailboat, Lee Clymer in the pilot helmet, Pricilla Minnich with the doll, and two other unidentified boys.

Children of Hess's employees have their own Cold War–era junior summit conference around 1962. The world's leaders of the Soviet Union, Cuba, France, Great Britain, and the United States are represented at Hess's Halloween promotion.

Hotpants and high boots were all the rage in the early 1970s when the Pennsylvania state lottery made its debut at Hess's. The young man in the Beatle haircut was then Lehigh Valley state representative Kurt D. Zwikl.

Hess's wooden soldiers became a part of the stores Christmas theme in the 1970s. They appeared at the South Mall store as a part of the Mickey Mouse and the 12 Toy Soldiers theme.

Here is a close up of the wooden soldiers. They were acquired for the store by Wolfgang Otto, a vice president of Hess's and a master of window display and design.

The Easter holiday was never neglected by Hess's. This photograph from the late 1940s shows Hamilton Street flooded with parents and children waiting to get a look at the bunny.

Yugoslav artist Jovan Obican was at Hess's in the 1970s. He was one of many artists attracted to Hess's by Philip I. and Muriel Berman.

Drew Pearson (center), noted syndicated political columnist for the *Washington Post* from the 1940s to the 1980s and whose column appeared regularly in the *Allentown Morning Call*, is shown autographing books at Hess's in the 1960s. The man to the right of Pearson is Hess's executive Bill Minnich.

Francoise Gilot, mistress and muse to Picasso, is shown with a Hess's executive at Hess's art gallery in the 1970s.

Political writer Jerry Bruno is shown being interviewed at Hess's at the debut of his book *The Advance Man* with Hess's public relations man Boris Weisman. During his career, Bruno headed advance teams that prepared public appearances for Pres. John F. Kennedy, Pres. Lyndon B. Johnson, Vice Pres. Hubert Humphrey, and Sen. Robert F. Kennedy.

Max Hess Jr. (fourth from left) was as firm a believer in the value of community service as his father, and he was often recognized for it. Here he is being given an award by the Pennsylvania Association of Professional Baseball Leagues around 1960 at Breadon Field, soon to be renamed Max Hess Stadium. Also pictured are Allentown mayor Donald Hock, at the far left, and Gov. David Lawrence, to the left of Hess.

Pictured here is an aerial view of Max Hess Stadium, which was begun as Breadon Field for the Allentown Cardinals, a farm team for the St. Louis Cardinals, in 1947. It was acquired by Hess in 1960.

Hess was a man who respected people of all faiths. Here he is in the early 1960s with Rev. Joseph McShea, bishop of the Roman Catholic diocese of Allentown. McShea is presenting Hess with a zucchetto, the small, round hat worn by Catholic clergy that belonged to Pope John XXIII, whose picture hangs on the wall behind them.

Philip I. Berman (left), who acquired the store from Hess in 1968, is shown in the early 1970s with local congressmen Fred Rooney. Berman had many friends in the political world, and they often came as his guest to Hess's.

State senator John (Johnny) Van Sandt (left) is presenting a proclamation from the state legislature to Philip I. Berman. Berman was often honored for the many charitable and other good works he performed for the store and the community.

One of the major events that Max Hess Jr. launched was Teen Trip of a Lifetime. It offered a young teenage girl a trip to some exotic locale. It also helped promote the store and attracted a great deal of good will. Here is Hess's teen trip award winner Suzanne Lechner shaking hands with actor Charlton Heston in the mid-1960s in Rome. Heston was there making the film *The Agony and the Ecstasy*, a fictional biography of the artist Michelangelo.

Teen Trip of a Lifetime winner Sally Ann Bowers is shown outside of Copenhagen in 1967. In addition to her trip, she modeled Denmark's latest fashion for *Ingenue* magazine.

Tower Bridge in London was the setting for this photograph of Stephanie Sikorski on the teen trip tour of 1965.

Gov. John Burns of Hawaii is presented with a Liberty Bell by Hess's teen trip winner Martha Sheska in 1968. The Liberty Bell model Sheska is giving Burns was symbolic of the original hidden in Allentown during the American Revolution while the British occupied Philadelphia.

Hess's flower shows of the 1960s were eye-popping spectaculars, featuring exotic plants from all corners of the globe. This photograph shows Oasis at Timbuktu, as cactus and other desert plants seem to float over the tie racks in the men's department.

Along with the exotic flowers that were a part of the Hess's flower show was the effective use of their reflections in mirrors, making the displays seem even more lavish and spectacular than they were. This display was known as Colorful Copenhagen and featured flowers from northern Europe, a quarter-million blooms.

Alluring Africa was the theme of this Hess's flower show display where Spanish carnations, Algerian snapdragons, and African daisies are among the flowers on display.

Another floral visit to northern Europe is called Sensational Scandinavia, which shows a mix of Dutch amaryllis, Scandinavian pinks, and French hydrangeas. Hess's magnificent chandeliers and mirrors added to the effect.

Casbah at Casablanca evoked the country of Morocco with a wide variety of flowers, including African snapdragons and Moroccan cornflowers. Who could resist buying something in a display out of the Arabian nights?

Hess's took off to the West Indies for this display, titled Antilles Calypso. Bird of paradise flowers and mauve orchids were the focal point of this display.

Polynesian Seas was the title of this display, featuring rain forests, fig trees, Fiji palms, and pineapple plants. It gave people in the Lehigh Valley a taste of the exotic that many of them had read about but never had a chance to see.

Raggedy Ann, tigers, and Santa Claus top this Hess's Christmas float clearly labeled as Hess's in the 1960s.

Here Hess's Wolfgang Otto (far left) is shown recognizing high school students for decorating in the 1970s in the store's parking garage.

Design students take a hand at creating a Three Kings Christmas display for Hess's parking garage in the 1970s.

The country's bicentennial was big all over America in 1976, and some Lehigh Valley students have included it in a Christmas display on Hess's parking deck.

Philip I. Berman (far right), Hess's owner from 1968 to 1980, is shown at an award ceremony for longtime Hess's employees. Future president Irwin Greenberg is at left and photographer Bill Zwikl is next to Berman. Note Hess's logo on the awards.

This Hess's service truck from the 1950s shows how the Hess's name was used in that era.

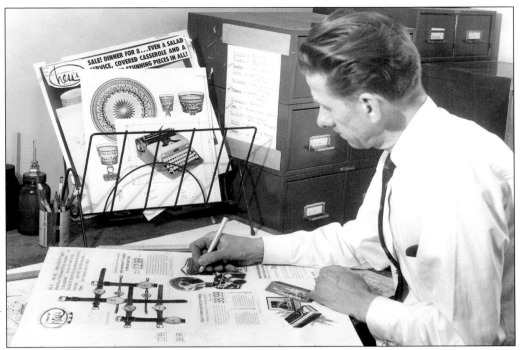

Zwikl, Hess's artist and staff photographer, is shown doing a layout for a Hess's newspaper advertisement in the 1960s. The name Hess's had already replaced Hess Brothers by that time.

Hess Brothers was the logo used on this Hess's delivery truck around 1959 or 1960.

As Hess's photographer, Bill Zwikl was called on to use many of his talents. Here in a self-portrait, he is shown setting up an advertising photograph.

Six

THE POLITICIANS

In the 1970s, Hess's new owner, Philip I. Berman, welcomed many politicians. Among them was Indiana senator Birch Bayh. This photograph was taken at a private party at the Berman's home in 1971. Bayh was testing the waters for a run for the Democratic presidential nomination in 1972.

Congressmen Wilbur Mills, chairman of the House Ways and Means Committee, is shown at Hess's in the early 1970s. He would later be forced to leave Congress due to scandal, but not before he tried to be drafted for president or vice president at the Democratic convention. Mills is speaking in the Patio Restaurant. Standing behind him is Hess's public relations man Boris Weisman.

Murial Humphrey, wife of vice president Hubert Humphrey, is shown speaking at Hess's in the spring of 1972. The Humphreys and the Bermans were close friends, and she came to Hess's at the Berman's request to campaign for her husband.

U.S. senator from Washington State Henry Scoop Jackson and his wife were guests of Hess's in 1975 when Jackson hoped to be the Democratic nominee for president the following year.

Dick Thornburgh, future governor of Pennsylvania, speaks with Allentown Public Library director Katherine Stephanoff while campaigning at Hess's in 1978.

Pennsylvania governor Raymond Shafer campaigns in Hess's Patio Restaurant and talks to potential voters in 1966. Shafer was a friend to both Max Hess Jr. and Philip I. Berman and often came to Hess's while visiting the Lehigh Valley.

Milton Shapp, left, campaigning to be the governor of Pennsylvania in 1970, is shown here shaking hands with Hess's owner Philip I. Berman.

Future president of the United States Jimmy Carter meets guests at a private reception at Hess's while running in the Pennsylvania primary in 1976. The man with the beard is Robert Rodale, head of Rodale natural foods and publications business. *Allentown Morning Call* owner Donald P. Miller is at lower right. Behind Carter is Ann Daddona, wife of Allentown mayor Joseph Daddona, and the man with the camera is Hess's photographer, Bill Zwikl.

Berman welcomes Carter to Hess's during the 1976 campaign for Pennsylvania's Democratic primary and introduces him at a private event for Hess's employees and community leaders. Hess's vice president Steve Furst is at right. Carter was elected president seven months later.

Jimmy Carter speaks to a crowd at Hess's while running for president in 1976.

Well-wishers and curious folks take time out to greet Carter as he strolls through Hess's main floor in the spring of 1976.

Hubert Humphrey, vice president and 1968 Democratic presidential candidate, walks through Hess's during the summer of 1968. To the right is Maggie Levine, longtime public relations man for Hess's, and next to Humphrey on the left is then Lehigh Valley congressman Fred Rooney.

Humphrey is set to address a crowd at Hess's after being introduced by Hess's president Philip I. Berman who is seen wearing an HHH campaign button.

After his campaign address, Hubert Humphrey takes time to mingle with Hess's coworkers and pose for a few photographs with a youngster in the store. Humphrey and Jimmy Carter made history as the highest-ranking officials to appear at Hess's.

Humphrey campaigns outside of Hess's in 1968 when he was running for president. Note the woman at left wearing a hat supporting Humphrey's Democratic rival Eugene McCarthy.

Hawaii congresswoman Patsy Mink and an unidentified man arrive at Allentown, Bethlehem Easton Airport. Mink was a guest of honor at one of Hess's flower shows that drew thousands of visitors to the store. Mink, who held a number of public positions, served 12 terms in the U.S. House of Representatives. She was also the first woman elected to Congress from Hawaii.

Alabama senator and 1952
Democratic vice presidential
nominee John Sparkman
participates in a Washington,
D.C., reception to promote
Pennsylvania-produced
products sponsored by Hess's.

Lillian Carter, the mother of Pres.
Jimmy Carter, addresses a crowded
Hess's reception in an effort to get
votes for the president's reelection
in 1980.

Joan Mondale shakes hands on Hess's main floor just before the November 1976 presidential election. She was the wife of Walter Mondale, Minnesota senator and vice presidential running mate of Jimmy Carter. Carter and Mondale were successfully elected. Hess's president Philip I. Berman is seen in the background.

Former Pennsylvania governor George Leader, a member of the board of directors of Hess's department stores, poses for a portrait in Hess's photograph department.

Seven

ENTERTAINING
TELEVISION AND
MOVIE STARS AND
OTHER CELEBRITIES

Philip I. Berman and his wife, Murial (in the foreground), were a significant presence in the Lehigh Valley long before he took over Hess's in 1968. Here they are shown as the prominent art collectors they were with a sculpture at their home in the 1970s.

The Berman's home, filled with modern art, was often the setting for fashionable parties. Here the artist Picasso's former mistress Francoise Gilot, in a pants suit (left), is being entertained with her husband, Jonas Salk, who developed polio's Salk vaccine, along with Allentown mayor Joseph Daddona (right) under the painting.

Guests at the party marveled at the Berman's art collection both inside and outdoors and in their library. After the Berman's death, their home on Lehigh Parkway was demolished, suffering the same fate as the department store at Ninth and Hamilton Streets.

Max Hess Jr. leaned more toward show business folks than artists. Here is a 1950s photograph of the Easter bunny welcoming television's Lassie, her master Jeff the actor Tommy Rettig, and Jon Hall, star of the popular show *Ramar of the Jungle*. Hall is placing Davy Crockett's coon-skin cap on Rettig's head.

Xavier Cugat, Cuban American band leader who helped introduce Latin music to the United States, shows off a sketch of Hess's executive Wayne Holben in the early 1960s. Cugat and his then wife, Abbe Lane, were often at Hess's and, in 1959, helped introduce the hula hoop there.

Many famous guests ate at Hess's Patio Restaurant. Here it plays host to television's Superman George Reeves (left) in 1956. Reeves is out of costume in this shot, but he seems to be enjoying himself while dining with Hess's executives.

Television actor Clint Walker is shown with Sally and Wayne Holben, the children of Hess's executive Wayne Holben, at a 1950s party for Walker at the Holben's home in Allentown's West End.

Max Hess Jr. loved the spotlight and being around television and movie stars. This classic photograph from about 1962 shows Hess with young *Tonight Show* host Johnny Carson (second from right), his sidekick Ed McMahon (right), and his orchestra leader Skitch Henderson, with the beard.

Hollywood heartthrob from the Doris Day *Pillow Talk* films of the early 1960s, Rock Hudson talks to some Hess's shoppers around 1962. Stars of Hudson's caliber were often part of the scene at Hess's.

Barbara Eden of *I Dream of Genie* television fame emerges from behind a vase at Hess's flower show in the 1960s. Eden was among the many celebrities that Hess's got to showcase its flower show event.

Zsa Zsa Gabor was not a major Hollywood talent, but she did have a big personality. Here she is in the 1960s hosting one of Hess's famous flower shows.

Dan Blocker (left) and Lorne Green were giants of 1960s television, with their hugely popular *Bonanza* Western program. Here they are in Hess's Patio Restaurant being served the store's legendary strawberry pie.

Efrem Zimbalist Jr. is not well remembered today, but in the late 1950s and early 1960s, he was the lead star in the highly popular detective television show *77 Sunset Strip*. Here he is during an appearance at Hess's, talking to the children of one of the store's executives.

Eddie Albert, the back-to-the-land husband of Eva Gabor in *Green Acres*, was also widely known for his roles in movies and as a stand-up comedian. Here he is making an appearance at Hess's in the 1960s.

122

Troy Donahue was a popular star of television and movies in the 1960s, and in the 1970s, he became a soap opera star. Here he is getting fitted for a rather exotic jacket with an Indian elephant design in Hess's men's department in the early 1960s.

Long before Tiger Woods, golfer Arnold Palmer (left) was a household name both on and off the putting green. He is shown here at Hess's with the store's public relations executive Maggie Levine during an appearance in the 1960s.

Wyatt Earp, also known as Hugh O'Brian, is shown out of the cowboy duds he wore on his popular 1950s television show named for the 19th-century Western lawman and in a stylish suit during an early-1960s appearance at Hess's. The lady with O'Brian is unidentified.

Max Hess Jr. loved to include his executives in on the act when a celebrity came to town. Here James Garner in cowboy hat, star of the popular 1960s television Western show *Maverick* and later *The Rockford Files* is shown playing cards with several of them in an appearance at the store in the 1960s.

Chuck Conners, the star of television's popular program *The Rifleman* was a hero to boys of all ages in the 1960s. Here young Kurt D. Zwikl and his childhood friend Peter Moggio admire the rapid-fire weapon that Conners used on the program during a 1960s appearance at Hess's.

Hess's also had many veteran actors stop in. Among them was Pat O'Brien, who began making films in the 1930s and is best remembered for his role of Notre Dame football coach Knute Rockne. O'Brien was also in a number of television programs in the 1960s and may have been appearing at Hess touting *Harrigan and Son*, a program about father and son lawyers that was on television from 1960 to 1961.

BIBLIOGRAPHY

Hall, Liz Armstrong. "Max Hess Jr. Puts Allentown on the Map." *Pennsylvania Heritage*, Vol. 30. Pennsylvania Historical and Museum Commission, Fall 2004.

Hellerich, Mahlon H. *Allentown, 1762–1987: A 225-Year History*. Allentown, PA: Lehigh County Historical Society, 1987.

Hess, Max Jr. *Every Dollar Counts: The Story of the American Department Store*. New York: Fairchild Publications, 1952.

"Hess's The Glory Days." *Allentown Morning Call*, February 1996, special section.

Hollywood on Hamilton Street: Remembering Hess's. Bethlehem, PA: PBS 39 WLVT, 2004.

Pierce-Jones, Gwen, "The Wonderful World of Hess's," *Proceedings of the Lehigh County Historical Society*, Vol. 43. Allentown, PA: Lehigh County Historical Society, 2002.

Zwikl, William R. *Taking Pictures*. Easton, PA: Hugh Moore Historical Park and Museums Center for Canal History and Technology, 1989.

Discover Thousands of Local History Books
Featuring Millions of Vintage Images

Arcadia Publishing, the leading local history publisher in the United States, is committed to making history accessible and meaningful through publishing books that celebrate and preserve the heritage of America's people and places.

Find more books like this at
www.arcadiapublishing.com

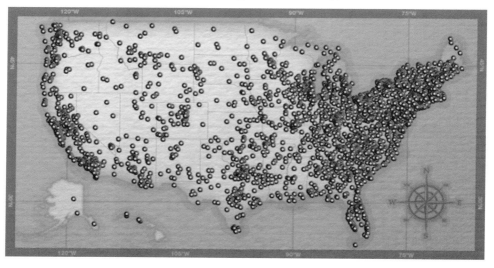

Search for your hometown history, your old stomping grounds, and even your favorite sports team.

Consistent with our mission to preserve history on a local level, this book was printed in South Carolina on American-made paper and manufactured entirely in the United States. Products carrying the accredited Forest Stewardship Council (FSC) label are printed on 100 percent FSC-certified paper.

MADE IN THE

USA